ROCKING IN INTELLECTUAL PROPERTY

ROCKING IN INTELLECTUAL PROPERTY

By: Andrew Abramson, Esq., Patent Attorney

Patent Profiler®, LLC

www.patentprofiler.com

The information in this e-book is not legal advice. If you need legal advice, please consult an attorney. Further, the information in this e-book is solely the opinion of the author and is for informational purposes only. This e-book should not be viewed as legal advice.

By providing names and/or links to other websites, Patent Profiler, LLC does not guarantee, approve, or endorse the information or products available at those sites, nor does a link indicate any association with or endorsement by the linked site to Patent Profiler, LLC.

1st Edition
Copyright 2020-2030. All rights reserved.

ANDREW ABRAMSON

1. Introduction to Intellectual Property................... pgs. 5 – 6
2. Copyrights ……………………………………….............. pgs. 7 – 14
3. Trade Secrets …….………………………………………….. pgs. 15 – 18
4. Trademarks ……………………….…………………………. pgs. 19 – 27
5. Patents …………………………………………….…… pgs. 28 – 41

1. INTRODUCTION TO INTELLECTUAL PROPERTY

Intellectual property (IP) is a valuable asset for any company. Often, the only way a small business can compete with the Goliaths of the world is through their intellectual property. Intellectual property takes many forms, such as copyrights, trade secrets, trademarks, and patents.

The strongest form of intellectual property is a patent. A patent protects an invention and provides a patent owner with a monopoly for a limited amount of time. As a patent is the strongest form of intellectual property, it has to be registered and is the most expensive to obtain and keep. The next strongest form of intellectual property is a trademark. A trademark protects a word or words, slogan, logo, etc. used to identify the source or origin of a good or product.

The trademark, which may be registered, is not as expensive as a patent but is rather moderately priced. A copyright protects a work of expression fixed in a tangible medium, such as a painting painted on a piece of paper. A copyright may be registered and protects against copying. There are nominal expenses to obtain a copyright. A trade secret protects information that provides a competitive advantage to its owner. A trade secret is not registered and lasts indefinitely (as long as it remains a secret).

    This e-book provides an introduction to the different forms of IP. No previous knowledge or experience on any of these topics is needed to understand what is covered in this e-book, so read on!

2. COPYRIGHTS

Copyrights protect works of expression recorded in some concrete way (also referred to as being fixed in a tangible medium). Copyright law covers the broad range of literary and artistic expression, including books, poetry, song, dance, dramatic works, computer programs, movies, sculptures, and paintings. Examples include an artist's painting on a canvas, a musician's song lyrics written on paper, a singer recording a song on a compact disc, an author's story being written on paper (e.g., in a book), someone developing and storing in a computer memory a web page or software code, etc.

The focus of copyright protection is originality of a work expressed or fixed in a tangible medium (e.g., paper, a canvas, a CD, a tape, computer memory, etc.). Ideas themselves are not copyrightable, but the author's particular expression of an idea is protectable under copyrights. A copyright protects the expression of a work and not the idea itself. For example, suppose I create a unique form (Form 1 below) with a particular layout and specific blanks for someone's name, occupation, and gender. If someone else creates a different form (Form 2) with a different layout but that has these same blanks, my copyright has not been infringed (which means violated) because the expression of this form (the layout) is different. The idea of having blanks for someone's name, occupation, and gender is not protected under copyright.

```
┌─────────────────────┐  ┌─────────────────────────┐
│  Form 1             │  │  Form 2                 │
│                     │  │                         │
│   ✗ ─────           │  │  Name _____ │
│                  │  │                         │
│                     │  │  Gender _____ │
│  Name _____ │  │                         │
│                     │  │  Occupation _____  │
│  Occupation _____  │  │                         │
│                     │  │         ◯               │
│  Gender _____  │  │                         │
│                     │  │                         │
│   ╱                 │  │                         │
└─────────────────────┘  └─────────────────────────┘
```

a. Obtaining a copyright

A copyright is easy to obtain and lasts longer than patent rights, but is narrower in scope than patents. Once a work is fixed in a tangible medium, a copyright attaches to the work. Thus, unlike patents and (federally registered) trademarks, which require examination and granting by the U.S. Patent and Trademark Office, no formal copyright registration is necessary to obtain a copyright. Therefore, once you create a work and fix it in a tangible medium, you can write on the work that it is copyrighted and the year that you created the work. For example, if you
develop a web page, you can write on the bottom of the web page "Copyrighted 2015. All rights reserved." This provides notice to people that you have a copyright in your web page and provides the first date of publication (here, 2015). Although this copyright notice is not required, it may be beneficial to you if you ever got into a disagreement with someone about the copying of your work.

Although not required, you can register a copright with the Copyright Office (www.copyright.gov). There are several benefits to registering your copyright with the Copyright Office.

These include:

1) Registration establishes a public record of the copyright claim.
2) Before you can sue someone for violating or infringing your copyright, registration is necessary.
3) If made before or within five years of publication, registration will establish evidence in court that your copyright is valid.
4) You may be awarded more money by a court if you sue someone for infringing your copyright and win.

Registration of a work with the Copyright Office is relatively inexpensive (e.g., between $35 -

$200). The Copyright Office does not "examine" or review / check applications for copyright and it does not "issue" copyrights. Rather, an author can only register their work with the Copyright Office. A copyright is protectable when it is created.

Additionally, creativity does not need to be present for a copyright to apply to a work. A copyright can apply to any original work expressed or fixed in a tangible medium. No one will judge your work as not being creative enough to warrant obtaining a copyright. Copyrights protect the copying of the work of expression and so if two people create very similar paintings independently, no copyright infringement has occurred. Facts themselves, however, cannot be protected by copyright.

b. Time period awarded by copyright protection

In the United States, most existing works have a copyright for a term ending 70 years after the death of the author. If the work was a work for hire (e.g., a work created by an employee of a corporation within the scope of the employee's employment, in which case the corporation is awarded the copyright), then the copyright lasts for 120 years after creation or 95 years after publication, whichever is shorter. As stated above, an author obtains a copyright once the work of expression is materialized in a tangible medium.

c. Work Made for Hire

As stated above, if a work was a work made for hire (also referred to as a "work for hire"), the work was created by an employee of a corporation within the scope of the employee's employment. Unless there is a written agreement to the contrary, the employer is awarded the copyright. Classifying a work as a work made for hire affects the initial ownership of the copyright and the copyright's duration. A work made for hire is typically a work created by an employee or a specially ordered or commissioned work that is subject to the supervision and control of the hiring party. A work created by an individual may or may not be a work for hire, depending on the type of work, the type of control the employer has over the work, any written agreement between the employer and individual, and employment factors between the individual and the employer (e.g., the duration of the relationship, the location of the work, the method of payment, the provision of employee benefits, the tax treatment of the individual, etc.). Thus, someone who is working for your company may or may not create a work for hire, regardless of whether you label the person as an employee or independent contractor. Courts will typically look at the above noted factors to determine if the person created a work for hire.

As an example of work for hire, many programmers created Microsoft Windows®, but the copyright in the software belongs to Microsoft®. Similarly, a newspaper owns the copyright in news articles written by its authors.

d. Rights Conferred by a Copyright

A copyright actually awards several rights, as described below.

i. Copying

The owner of a copyright has the exclusive right to make copies of his work. Thus, a copyright protects against copying of protected expression. An independent creation of a work that is similar to a copyrighted work is not subject to the copyright.

ii. Derivative Works

The owner of a copyright has the exclusive right to prepare "derivative works". A derivative work is a work based on the original work but in a different form or otherwise changed or adapted in some manner. For example, a movie based on a book, a translation, a sound recording, etc. are derivative works. These derivative works are also copyrightable.

A "compilation" is a work formed by the collection and assembling of preexisting materials or of data that are selected, coordinated, or arranged in such a way that the resulting work as a whole constitutes an original work of authorship. An example is an encyclopedia because an encyclopedia contains a number of independent works assembled into a collective whole. A compilation can be copyrighted if there is some minimal degree of creativity to merit copyright protection.

iii. Distribution

The owner of the copyright has the right to control the sale and distribution of the original work and any copies or derivative works. This right only extends to the first sale of the works and does not apply to additional sales. For example, if I am an artist and I paint a picture, I can sell the picture to person A for a price that I set. I cannot, however, prohibit person A from selling the picture to person B. Similarly, I cannot set the price that person A sells the picture for to person B.

iv. Performance and Display

The owner of a copyright has the right to control the public (but not private) performance and display of the copyrighted work. This does not relate to using a receiving apparatus that is basically a private home-type device, such as a radio or television. Thus, a restaurant or hotel that plays music through speakers for its guests is not infringing the copyright in the music being played.

e. Infringement of a copyrighted work

An infringement of a copyrighted work occurs when someone copies the work. To determine if a work has been copied illegally, courts accept proof that a party had access to the copyrighted work (such as that the copyrighted work was displayed on a web page). The courts usually also look at evidence indicating that the two works are substantially similar.

A copyrighted work would be infringed by copying the entire work or copying a substantial part of the work. Even the copying of a small amount of the original work, if significant in quality, may be enough for infringement of the original work.

If a first artist paints a new painting that is substantially similar to another painting made by a second artist but that has not yet been released to the public, most courts would determine that no copyright infringement has occurred because the first artist independently created the painting without having access to the second artist's painting. A copying has to be inferred or directly proven for copyright infringement to be found.

f. Defense to Copyright Infringement – Fair Use

If someone copies a copyrighted work, he is typically infringing the copyright. There is, however, a defense to the claim of copyright infringement – fair use. If the copying is fair use, then the person who copied the original work does not infringe the copyright and does not have to obtain permission from or pay the author of the original work. Fair use can include reproduction for criticism, news reporting, education (including making multiple copies for classroom use), scholarship, or research.

The factors to consider when determining whether a use of a work is fair use include:

1) The purpose and character of the use;
2) The nature of the copyrighted work;
3) The amount and substantiality of the portion used in relation to the entire copyrighted work; and
4) The effect of the use upon the potential market for or value of the copyrighted work.

With respect to the first factor, the purpose and character of the use, courts may look at whether the use is of a commercial nature or is for nonprofit educational purposes and/or the public benefit of the use. With respect to the second factor, the nature of the copyrighted work, courts typically determine that there is a greater need to distribute factual works than works of fiction or fantasy. With respect to the third factor, the amount and substantiality of the copied portion, courts look at how much of the original was taken and how valuable the copied portion is to the entire work. With respect to the fourth factor, the effect of the use upon the potential market for the copyrighted work, courts typically look at whether there is a substantial harm to the value of the copyright due to the copying. A court will typically look at these factors and weigh them together to determine whether the copying of an original work constitutes a fair use.

One example of a fair use is a parody. A parody is a work that makes fun of an original work through imitation and distortion. As people need to recognize the connection between the original work and the parody, the parody copies at least some of the original work. A Saturday Night Live skit in which an actor sings a distorted version of a famous (copyrighted) song is an example of a parody because the skit copies some of the famous (copyrighted) song but distorts it to make it humorous. Saturday Night Live is not infringing the copyright in the original song because the SNL song is a parody and therefore constitutes fair use.

g. Strategy for best practices

I recommend fixing your work in a tangible medium, which is easy to do. I also recommend marking your work with a copyright notice and the year of first publication. For example, if you develop a web site and publish the site in 2014, put on the bottom of each page "Copyright 2014. All rights reserved."

As registering your copyright with the Copyright Office is relatively inexpensive, I recommend doing this so that you obtain the benefits of registration.

3. TRADE SECRETS

A trade secret is any information used in one's business that gives the business owner a competitive advantage over others who do not know the information. Thus, a trade secret is any valuable information not generally known that adds or is capable of adding economic value to the owner. A trade secret can be a formula, practice, process, method, technique, design, instrument, pattern, or compilation of information which is confidential and is not easily obtainable.

Unlike patents, which expire after a certain period of time, trade secret protection lasts indefinitely as long as the information remains a secret. The formula for Coke® is a classic example. The Coca-Cola® Company does not have a patent on the formula for Coke® but instead relies on trade secret protection to protect this valuable formula.

If someone acquires your trade secret wrongfully (also referred to as trade secret misappropriation), you can sue them. Misappropriation of a trade secret includes acquiring the information through deception, theft, spying, etc.

The key to keeping a trade secret is to perform steps or execute procedures to keep the information secret. An example of a procedure to keep information secret includes when a company only allows a few key people to know the secret (disclosure of a trade secret to a limited extent (e.g., to a few people) does not destroy its status as a trade secret). Another example is when a company secures the information (e.g., formula) in a safe, vault, secure room, or secure area. If no procedures are in place to keep the information confidential, a company cannot later state that the information is a trade secret. Once a trade secret is lost, the owner of the information cannot prevent others from copying or using the trade secret.

a. Preexisting obligation to keep information secret

A party's use or disclosure of information can be wrongful due to a preexisting obligation of the party. This preexisting obligation usually occurs due to an explicit or implied contract or duty. For example, you may sign a contract stating that you cannot disclose confidential information that you have learned. This contract may be an employment agreement, which is often signed at the start of your employment with a company. During the course of your employment, if you learn of confidential information, you may not be able to disclose this information as stated in the contract, even after your employment with the company ends.

An example of an implied contract or duty is when a company hires an employee. Even without an explicit contract, courts have ruled that employees typically have to keep their employer's confidential information a secret, assuming the company treats the information as a secret and maintains and implements procedures to protect the information. Even after an employee leaves the company, the employee usually has to keep the learned trade secret confidential. Former employees are, however, allowed to take with them the general knowledge, skill, training, and experience that they obtained from working at the company.

b. Disclosure of Trade Secret

The protection of a trade secret continues indefinitely as long as the trade secret remains secret. Thus, a public disclosure of a trade secret destroys the secret and therefore ends trade secret protection.

An example of a disclosure of a trade secret is when the trade secret owner publishes the secret (e.g., at a conference, in an article, on a web page, etc.). Taking this example further and as described in more detail below, filing a patent application on an advancement usually destroys trade secret protection for that advancement because patent applications usually publish after a certain amount of time. Similarly, if and when a patent issues, the patent is published. Thus, a company cannot have a patent on an invention and also keep it a trade secret. Once the patent application or patent publishes, the trade secret is lost.

Another example of a disclosure of a trade secret (and therefore the elimination of trade secret protection) is when the secret is disclosed by selling a product that reveals the trade secret. If, however, the trade secret is contained in an undiscoverable form within a product and the product is sold, trade secret protection for the secret is not lost. This applies, for instance, with object code of a computer program because the object code does not reveal the actual computer program.

A third example of a disclosure of a trade secret is when a third party who is not the owner of the trade secret finds out about the secret (such as by stealing the secret) and then publishes the information. Even though the company did not publish the information, the information is no longer a secret and trade secret protection is lost. The company will likely be able to sue and win against the third party for trade secret misappropriation, but the trade secret protection will be lost for that information.

c. Reverse Engineering

A legitimate obtaining of a trade secret occurs through reverse engineering. Thus, buying a competitor's product and taking it apart to learn how the product is made or to learn of its components is legal. The owner of the trade secret used to make the product cannot sue the party for reverse engineering the trade secret, as no misappropriation of the trade secret has occurred. Thus, if I develop a product using a trade secret and sell this product to you, you can legally reverse engineer the product to determine the trade secret (if possible). If you successfully reverse engineer the product and then publish the secret (e.g., on a web page, in an article, etc.), I cannot sue you for misappropriation of the trade secret because you obtained the trade secret lawfully.

d. Strategy for best practices

Trade secrets are extremely valuable, as the rights exist indefinitely while the information remains a secret. If you have obtained valuable information that you want to secure as a trade secret, you must put procedures in place to keep the information confidential. I recommend putting the information in a locked safe, and only providing the password or key to a few select individuals. Also, if you have employees, make sure your employment agreement indicates that any confidential information obtained during the employee's employment with the company shall remain confidential and be treated as confidential. I would recommend consulting an employment attorney to review and revise your employment agreement, as this can become very important when trade secret rights are at issue.

4. TRADEMARKS

Trademarks are one or more words, graphics, logos, slogans, sounds, colors, and/or scents that identify a source or origin of a product or good. Trademark protection is awarded to those who are the first to use a distinctive mark in commerce.

An example is the Nike® Swoosh. To obtain a trademark, one may apply for the trademark with the U.S. Patent and Trademark Office (USPTO). The USPTO performs a search to see if any other marks exist that are too similar to the application. If there is a likelihood of confusion with another mark, the USPTO will reject the application. If you can convince the USPTO that your application should be granted, and if the USPTO does grant the application, the trademark is valid throughout the United States.

If you register your trademark, you obtain the right to exclusive use of the mark in relation to the products or services for which it is registered. Typically, the owner of a registered mark can prevent unauthorized use of the mark in relation to products or services which are identical or similar to the registered products or services. The test is always whether a consumer of the goods or services will be confused as to the identity of the source or origin.

a. Classification of Trademarks

> Only certain trademarks are afforded legal protection, depending on their classification.

A mark can be classified as either:

1) Arbitrary or fanciful,
2) Suggestive,
3) Descriptive, or
4) Generic.

An arbitrary or fanciful mark is a word, phrase, logo, etc. that does not describe or relate to the product associated with the mark. Arbitrary or fanciful marks are the strongest marks because they are recognized only due to the commercial use of the mark with a product. Examples of arbitrary or fanciful trademarks include Nike® for sneakers, the Nike® "swoosh" (below), Apple® for computers, the Apple® logo (below), Shell® for gasoline, and the Shell® logo (below).

As you move further down the list of classifications, the strength of the mark decreases. Suggestive marks suggest a product to people. Examples of suggestive marks are Microsoft® for software for a microcomputer and Coppertone® for sun tanning products. Descriptive marks describe the product or service offered. An example of a descriptive mark is ComputerLand® for a computer store. As stated below, descriptive marks do not become protectable trademarks unless secondary meaning is established. Generic marks are so entwined with the product that the mark has become the way people refer to that type of product. Examples of generic marks are Kleenex, aspirin and cellophane. Generic marks may have started out as arbitrary, suggestive, or descriptive, but, through years of use, they have become generic and have lost their rights as trademarks.

b.   Secondary Meaning

When a trademark immediately identifies a company, the legal rights to the mark are determined only through priority of use (i.e., who used the mark first with a product). To secure the rights in descriptive marks, however, secondary meaning must be present. Secondary meaning exists when people associate a product with a single source. Secondary meaning is usually established through long term use of a mark and/or a lot of publicity and advertising. Examples of descriptive marks that have obtained secondary meaning include Sharp® for televisions and Tender Vittles® for cat food.

c.   Registration of Trademark

You can register your trademark with the state you do business in (e.g., via the state's website, such as www.ny.gov or www.ma.gov) or you can register your trademark nationally via the USPTO.

There are several advantages to registering your mark nationally with the USPTO (also called a federal registration). A person who registers a mark with the USPTO has superior rights to use the registered mark throughout the United States compared with someone who registers a similar mark with a state (after the federal registration). This is true regardless of whether the person has been granted a state registration or was the first person to use the mark in the state.

For example, if Bob registers his mark with the USPTO and John then registers his mark in NY for a similar product, and if Bob decides to do business in NY, Bob will be able to use the nationally registered mark while John will have to stop using his mark. Thus, when there is a conflict between a federal registration and a state registration, the federal registration typically wins. John may continue to use his mark in NY for as long as Bob does not do business in NY. But once Bob decides to do business in NY, John must cease use of his mark. A federal registration provides Bob with the right to use his mark throughout the entire country (even if Bob is not currently using his mark in a specific geographic area) and Bob can prevent others from using the same or similar mark anywhere in the U.S.

An exception to this exists when the state mark was registered before the federal registration. If the state mark was in use before the date of first use of the federally registered mark, the prior state user may have some rights to use the mark, but those rights would be limited to the state where the mark has been registered and used. Thus, if John registered his mark in NY first and then Bob registered his mark with the USPTO, John could continue using his mark in NY even if Bob wanted to do business in NY because John registered first in NY.

To register a mark with the USPTO, the mark must be either used in commerce or registered with an intent to use in commerce. When you apply for a registration of a mark with the USPTO, you must identify the goods and/or services to which the mark will apply.

If you register a mark with an intent to use the mark in commerce, the USPTO will issue you a notice of allowance if the application for your mark is otherwise allowable. Once this notice of allowance is issued, the trademark owner has six months (extendable) to submit a statement that the trademark has in fact been used in commerce. If this statement is received, the mark will then be entered on the principal register. If the trademark owner does not submit such a statement, the trademark is considered abandoned. If your trademark becomes abandoned, you lose your rights in the mark and any party can use the mark.

You can also obtain a common law trademark through the use of a mark in a specific geographic area without registering the mark. For example, if John uses his mark in NY (without registering the mark in NY or with the USPTO) and John is the first to use this mark in NY, John obtains a "common law trademark". If Bob later registers a mark for a similar product with the USPTO, Bob has rights throughout the U.S. with his mark except for in NY where John uses his mark (and sells his product or advertises his product). John cannot, however, expand outside of NY, as Bob has rights in his mark throughout the rest of the U.S. If John puts up a web page and has customers in NY, FL, and CA, and these customers associate John's mark with his product, then John likely has common law trademark protection in these states.

The safest strategy, with the global reach of the Internet, is to register your mark with the USPTO after performing Internet searches for your mark and viewing these results in light of your product. You should also do a domain name search (e.g., on www.godaddy.com or www.networksolutions.com) for your trademark to make sure no one else has registered a domain name on your mark.

d. Marking a trademark

Certain symbols, when used in conjunction with a mark, provide notice to the public that the owner is claiming trademark rights in the word(s) before the symbol. Providing notice of a trademark may help an owner of a mark if the owner ever got into a litigation against a party that is infringing the owner's mark.

Specifically, the ® symbol tells the public that the mark is registered with the USPTO. You should use the ® symbol after your trademark once the trademark has completed registration with the USPTO (and not after just applying for the trademark). If a mark is not federally registered, the symbol ™ for "trademark" or ᔆᔐ for "service mark" can be used to indicate that, even though the mark is not registered, the owner is nonetheless claiming rights in it. The ™ symbol stands for "trademark" and is usually placed after and above the mark. The ᔆᔐ symbol stands for "service mark", which is the same as a trademark except that it identifies and distinguishes the source of a service rather than a good. I recommend using the ® symbol, ™ symbol or ᔆᔐ symbol on marks that appear on your product, packaging, print, advertising, instructions, etc. each time the mark is present on one of these items.

e. Trademark Infringement

Trademark infringement occurs when a company A uses a mark to identify its product or service and the mark is similar to or the same as a mark used by company B for a similar product or service. To determine if the company A's mark is "infringing" or violating company B's mark, a court would look at the following two criteria: (1) likelihood of confusion, and (2) dilution. A brief introduction to these two criteria follows.

i. Likelihood of Confusion

There are 8 factors that are considered in determining whether there is a likelihood of confusion between goods:
(1)   Similarity of the marks (including the marks' look, phonetic similarities, and underlying meanings);
(2)   Similarities of the goods and services involved

(including an examination of the marketing channels for the goods);
(3) The strength of the plaintiff's mark (i.e., the mark of the party who is suing);
(4) The physical proximity of the goods in the marketplace;
(5) Any evidence of actual confusion;
(6) Intent of the defendant in adopting its mark (i.e., the intent of the party being sued in adopting its mark);
(7) The degree of care likely to be exercised by the purchaser; and
(8) The likelihood of expansion of the product lines.

The first two factors are probably the most important in determining likelihood of confusion. All other things being equal, the more similar the mark, the more likely it is that confusion will exist.

With respect to the first factor, courts typically look at each mark as a whole to determine how similar they are to one another. The test involves the degree of similarity. When the mark is fanciful / arbitrary, less actual copying of each linguistic element is necessary for similarity to be found. Thus, if two fanciful marks are similar in many but not all respects (e.g., similar in sound), a court will typically find likelihood of confusion because the marks are fanciful / arbitrary. When the marks are not fanciful or arbitrary, courts are more likely to require greater similarity (e.g., of sound).

With respect to the second factor, marks that are nearly identical may be found noninfringing if they are used on entirely unrelated and dissimilar goods (or services). Similarity of goods or services is determined by looking at whether the products or services are viewed as similar to the average consumer. With respect to the third factor, the nature of the mark typically affects the strength of the mark (e.g., a fanciful or arbitrary mark will likely receive more protection than a common phrase). With respect to the fourth factor, the location of products having similar marks will typically help determine if a consumer would be confused by the two marks. With respect to the fifth factor, evidence of actual confusion of consumers between products bearing two different but similar marks helps determine that there is a likelihood of confusion between the marks. Courts may also look at intent of the defendant (person or company being sued) in adopting its mark, the degree of care likely to be exercised by the consumer, and/or the likelihood of expansion of the product lines associated with the similar marks.

ii. Dilution

There are five elements necessary for a claim of dilution:

(1) The first mark must be famous;
(2) It must be distinctive;
(3) The second use must be a commercial use in commerce;
(4) It must begin after the first mark has become famous; and (5) It must cause dilution of the distinctive quality of the first mark.

Once a trademark itself has acquired value, legal protection will not depend solely on th
likelihood of confusion as to the source. Trademarks can embody an owner's reputation and
goodwill. Thus, even if there is no likelihood of confusion between marks, a trademark owner may still be able to prevail if another party has "diluted" the mark (or lessened the strength of the mark). For example, if a product A has a similar or identical mark as a product B, and product A is inferior to product B, the owner of the mark associated with product B may have a dilution case due to consumers thinking less of the owner of product B.

f. Cybersquatting of domain names

Cybersquatting occurs when a person other than the

trademark holder registers the domain name of a well-known trademark and then attempts to profit from this by either ransoming the domain name back to the trademark holder or using the domain name to divert business from the trademark holder to the domain name holder. A person will be guilty of cybersquatting if he, without regard to the goods or services of the owner of the mark, (i) had a bad faith intent to profit from the mark; and (2) registers, traffics in, or uses a domain name that is confusingly similar to another's mark or dilutes another's mark.

g. Strategy for best practices

The strongest trademarks are fanciful or arbitrary marks. Try to name your company or product with a fanciful or arbitrary mark. Perform an Internet search for your name before registering your name. Search using Google, Yahoo! and the USPTO trademark search tool (www.uspto.gov), search for similar domain names, and/or search the state business name directories. Once you have done an exhaustive search, you can register your mark with the USPTO.

You may want to hire an attorney to apply for your mark, or you can apply for the mark yourself. Nonetheless, the safest strategy, with the global reach of the Internet, is to register your mark with the USPTO after performing Internet searches for your mark and viewing these results in light of your product. Also, try to use your mark in commerce (e.g., on your website) as an adjective with your product (e.g., Xerox® copiers). Doing this may prevent your mark from becoming generic (which would cause you to lose your trademark rights in the mark).

5. PATENTS

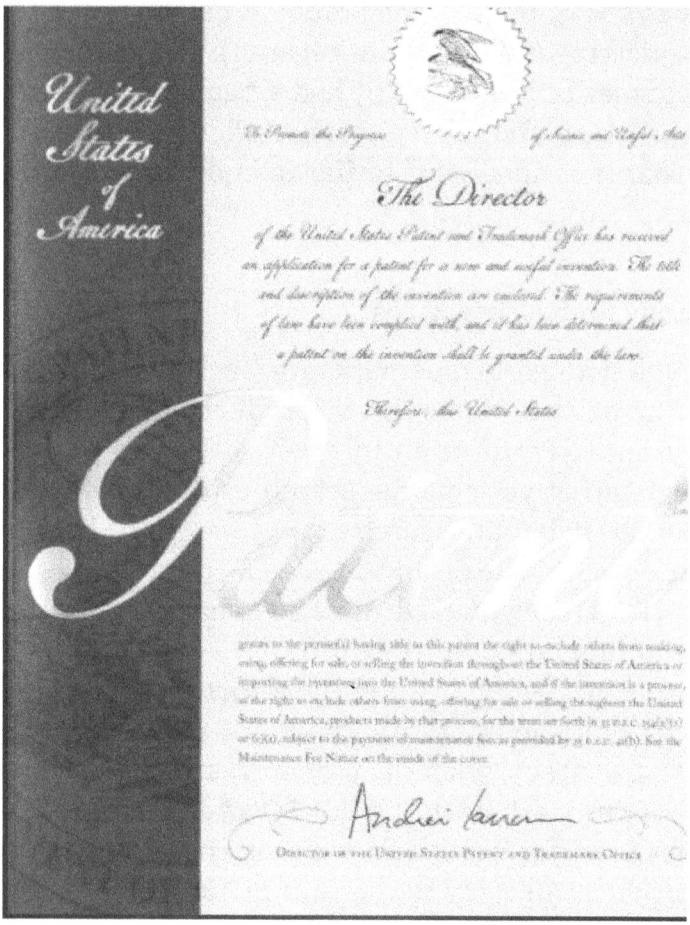

Patents are legal documents filed with the USPTO that describe and protect inventions.

Patents provide a negative right – the right to exclude others from making, selling, using, or importing the patented invention. People often think of a patent as a monopoly in the claimed invention for a limited period of time. Patents are valid for twenty years from the patent's filing date. In exchange for the monopoly granted by the U.S. government for a limited period of time, the patent is published so that others can learn from the patented invention and potentially build upon the knowledge.

The act of filing a patent application with the USPTO enables you to write on your product the words "patent pending". These words lend credibility to your product, may increase sales, and may cause competitors to think twice before copying your product. Additionally, you will have many more rights if you have a patent application on file with the USPTO than if you didn't file before you speak to a company about your product regarding manufacturing and/or selling your product. Also, if you ever need to speak to a potential investor to try to get funding for your business, the investor will usually ask if you have any patents or patent applications on file. Answering yes to these questions will typically help facilitate obtaining funding. Further, if you are granted a patent, you can prevent people from copying your invention. You can also license your invention to another company. This company can then make and sell a product based on your patent while you build your wealth by collecting royalties.

a. Requirements to Obtain a U.S. Patent

A patent application describes an invention. The invention has to be either a method, machine, article of manufacture, composition, or new use of one of these. As described above, the government effectively gives you a monopoly in your invention for a limited period of time.

Prior to March 16, 2013, in the U.S., an inventor could get a patent on an invention if the inventor was the first one to come up with the idea (the first inventor). On September 16, 2011, President Obama signed into law the America Invents Act (AIA). This law changed the U.S. from a first-to-invent country to a first-inventor-to-file country, and the change went into effect on March 16, 2013. This legislation in effect created a first-to-disclose patent system, where the first inventor to disclose the invention (e.g., through a public disclosure, a written article, or the filing of a patent application or provisional patent application) usually wins the race.

Specifically, an inventor has one year from the date of disclosure to file a patent application. In order to obtain a patent on an idea, the idea has to meet three requirements. The idea has to be novel or new, has to have utility or usefulness, and has to be non-obvious. Novelty is a comparison of what the idea is relative to what else is known prior to your earliest patent application filing date. Utility is a relatively easy standard to meet, as just about anything has utility. Nonobviousness is a tougher requirement to satisfy, as an invention can't be obvious in view of other known ideas or combination of ideas. Obviousness is viewed in light of "one of ordinary skill in the art" which is a fictitious person who is skilled in the technology described in the patent application.

After you file your patent application, you can argue to the USPTO that your invention is not obvious in light of other references (called "prior art") if the references do not teach or suggest your invention. You would highlight the differences in your invention over the teachings of the cited prior art. Factors that strengthen your case that your invention is not obvious include commercial success, long felt but unsolved needs, failures of others, and/or evidence that the claimed invention yields unexpected results or properties. Sometimes a small change in a method or system yields unexpected results and this small change would likely be considered non-obvious. Another example of a non-obvious invention is if every other product in an industry does something a specific way and your invention does the same thing in a different way. This difference would likely be considered non-obvious and patentable.

Almost any idea can be patented. For example, software, business methods, methods of manufacture, systems, apparatus, medical devices, algorithms, consumer products, and biotechnology can be patented. There are a few concepts, however, that cannot be patented. In particular, abstract ideas, natural phenomena, and laws of nature, such as the theory of relativity, cannot be patented.

B. ACTIONS THAT CAN AFFECT YOUR PATENT RIGHTS

There are a few actions that, if you perform, can negatively impact your patent rights. The first action is if you make your idea publicly available. For example, presenting your idea at a conference or in a poster, publishing your idea in a paper, or publishing your idea on a web site can affect your patent rights. Publishing your idea starts a one year clock in the U.S. You then have to file a patent application within that year. If you don't, you lose all rights in your idea.

The second action is selling your product or offering your product for sale. If you either sell the product that you would like to get a patent on or offer the product for sale to a potential customer, this may count as a disclosure and you may again start the clock running in the U.S. from the date of the sale or offer for sale. With an offer for sale, you don't even have to have a physical product – if you offer your product for sale by showing detailed drawings of how your product would be built or would work is likely enough to start the patent clock. You may then have one year from that date to file a patent application with the USPTO. This is known as the "on-sale bar". Although it is, at this time, somewhat unclear how the AIA treats the on-sale bar, this is likely considered a public disclosure by the inventor of the invention (in which case you would have one year to file a patent application). Courts have not yet decided on how the AIA treats the on-sale bar.

The third action that can negatively affect patent rights is if you use your product publicly (public use). For example, if you install your new gravel onto a road to make the road more resilient, this would likely start the clock running and you would have one year from this public use to file a patent application (because this is likely considered a public disclosure). There is, however, an exception to this rule. If your use is an experimental use, then the clock does not start. So, using the same example, if you are testing your gravel and are making changes to your gravel as cars go over the gravel over a period of time (and keeping records of these changes), then the clock would not start running because you are experimenting with your gravel and your invention has not been finalized. Once you stop experimenting, the clock would likely start.

If you do not file a patent application on or before that one year deadline, you lose all rights in your invention in the U.S. Speaking from experience, the year goes by quickly and often sneaks up on inventors. Also, as the law is somewhat unclear with the AIA changes, I recommend filing a patent application <u>before</u> one of these events occurs to be on the safe side.

In most foreign countries, you lose all of your patent rights if you publish your invention, sell or offer your invention for sale, or use your invention publicly before you file a patent application.

Once you file your patent application, you can discuss your product and/or sell your product freely. When trying to sell your product, a patent or patent application provides a big boost in the product's credibility. Additionally, if you discuss your product with a potential licensee or manufacturer, the patent or patent application can help facilitate the making of a deal with your product.

c. Steps to Get From Patent Pending to Issued Patent

Once you file a patent application, the journey is just beginning on being awarded a patent. As stated above, you can write the words "patent pending" on your product associated with the patent application. But how do you get to an issued patent? After a period of time, an examiner at the UPSTO will examine your patent application. Most of the time, they will send a communication back to you describing why they think your idea is not patentable. In this communication, which is called an Office Action, the examiner will typically refer you to different parts of other publications and say that these publications already show your idea.

Therefore, they will say, you cannot be awarded a patent because your idea is already known or is obvious in light of what is known. You have to respond to the USPTO's Office Action with a written response. If you can convince the Examiner that your idea is different than what they are pointing to, the Examiner will either issue a new Office Action or will award you a patent on your invention. The process of trying to get a patent, such as by arguing with the USPTO on the patentability of your invention, is called "prosecution" of a patent application.

d. Should I Do a Search on My Idea Before Filing a Patent Application?

A common question that I often hear from inventors is whether they have to or should perform a search for their idea before filing a patent application. Let's set the record straight - performing a search is not required before filing a patent application. You do not have to perform a single search on your idea before filing a patent application. It may, however, be beneficial to you to do a search before filing a patent application to determine what else is out there that is similar to your idea and to determine whether it makes sense for you to go forward with the filing of a patent application.

One caveat to searching patent applications for your idea is that patent applications publish 18 months after their filing date. Therefore, there may be patent applications that disclose your idea that have been filed but have not published yet. There is nothing you can do about this – it is a risk that you have to weigh before deciding to file your application.

Before drafting a patent application, you should thoroughly review the references you found to determine what you can patent. It may be helpful to take notes on each reference, such as writing down what the reference discloses, the problem or problems the reference solves, etc. You should focus your patent application on the patentable subject matter not disclosed in the references.

Also, remember during your searching that all inventions build upon what is known. You may locate references that disclose your broad invention, but don't get discouraged! You may have to change your view of what part of your idea is patentable, but sometimes the most valuable patents are patents that protect an incremental change in a specific area. Additionally, if you do decide to file a patent application after doing some searching, you will have to provide your relevant search results to the USPTO.

E. PROVISIONAL PATENT APPLICATION

As a small business or a solo inventor, you may not be sure whether you want to take the plunge and file a full-blown patent application (also called a utility patent application). You are not sure if your idea is patentable. Or you may not have perfected your idea and you may need more time to flesh out the details of your idea. Or you are not sure if your idea is marketable.

Instead of filing a utility patent application, you can file a placeholder patent application, also called a provisional patent application. You do get a filing date for the provisional application. A provisional patent application, however, must be converted into a utility patent application on or before its one year anniversary. If the one year anniversary ends on a weekend or holiday, you can file the utility patent application on the next business day. If you don't decide to convert the provisional patent application into a

utility patent application by the one year anniversary date of the provisional filing date, the provisional patent application expires and remains unknown (does not publish).

For example, suppose you file a provisional patent application on March 28, 2003. By March 28, 2004, you have to file a utility patent application that "claims priority" back to the provisional patent application to get the earlier filing date of the provisional application. If you do not file a utility patent application that claims priority back to the provisional patent application by the March 28, 2004 deadline, then the provisional patent application expires and is no longer in force.

A utility patent application has a specific format that it must follow. A provisional patent application, however, can have any format.

Provisional patent applications are relatively inexpensive. If you hire a patent attorney to prepare a provisional application for you, the cost is typically between $700 - $5000, depending on how much work goes into the application. If you prepare a provisional application and have a patent attorney review it for you, the costs will likely be less.

F. UTILITY PATENT APPLICATION

A utility patent application includes several parts – the specification, figures, claims, and abstract. The specification is the description of your invention, including a background section, a summary of your invention, and a detailed description of your invention. You should be aware that once you file your patent application, you cannot change or add to your specification (except to correct minor typographical errors). Therefore, it is important to be complete and thorough in your application. You should describe your invention in sufficient detail to enable one of ordinary skill in the art to make and use your invention after reading your application without much additional work.

The figures are one or more drawings that help describe your invention. Each figure should include reference numbers that point to a part of the drawing and that are referred to in your specification.

The claims are the sentences that define your invention. They are the legal metes and bounds of your invention. They are similar to a property deed to a house – they define the boundaries of your invention. The claims are supported by the specification and figures. To determine the meaning of claim terms, one initially looks at the specification and figures.

The patent application also includes an abstract. The abstract is at the end of the document and is mainly used for searching purposes. The abstract is typically a brief summary of your invention and must be 150 words or less.

Obtaining a patent is not cheap, as patents are the strongest form of intellectual property. To draft and file a utility patent application, patent attorneys typically charge between $9,000 -
$15,000, depending on the complexity of the invention. You can also draft a patent application yourself to lessen the attorney fees. You can then file the application yourself or have a patent attorney review and file your application. There are further costs after filing, such as preparing and filing one or more Responses to Office Actions as well as fees that need to be paid to the USPTO if and when the patent application issues as a patent.

G. INFRINGEMENT OF CLAIMS

Another party infringes a patented claim when they make, use, sell, or import the elements of the claim. For example, if a party performs the steps of the claim, and has the components, modules or parts that are claimed, they infringe the claim.

If you have a patent and want to assert one or more claims of the patent, you can choose which claim or claims to assert. If a competitor infringes a claim, you can often collect money from the infringer for infringing your patent. If the patent is involved in a lawsuit, the defendant usually states that your patent is invalid and unenforceable. The defendant will attempt to find prior art that discloses what you claim, thereby trying to indicate that your "invention" was already known before your filing date.

H. STRATEGY FOR BEST PRACTICES

If you think you have come up with an invention, I recommend doing some searching on the Internet first, such as on Google, Yahoo! and the USPTO web site. If you do not find anything that is exactly your invention, I next recommend preparing and filing a provisional patent application so that you have a placeholder application on file. Next, now that you have a year before you have to convert your provisional patent application into a utility patent application, I recommend developing a prototype of your invention (if possible) and contacting as many companies as possible in the field of your invention to discuss your invention to see if they would be willing to sell your invention or license your invention. After the year is up, if you have made progress, if you need more time, and/or if you still feel like you have a patentable invention, I would convert the provisional patent application into a full blown utility patent application.

Thank you! Please let us know what you thought of this book by emailing us at

general@patentprofiler.com

About the Author

Andrew Abramson is a registered patent attorney with over fifteen years of experience in patent application drafting and patent prosecution. Andrew has worked in both large law firms and a small law firm with just a few attorneys. Andrew has counseled and performed IP work for large corporations, medium-sized companies, universities, small companies, and solo inventors.

Andrew graduated from Suffolk University Law School, cum laude, with a concentration in Intellectual Property, with distinction. For the majority of his law school career, Andrew went to law school in the evening while working for a large law firm during the day. During his first year of law school, Andrew was ranked first in his class and also won the award for Best Legal Writing Brief. Andrew won the Carol DiMatti scholarship after his first year of law school.

Andrew also attended Binghamton University and graduated with a Bachelors of Science degree in Electrical Engineering. Andrew was a member of Eta Kappa Nu, the Electrical Engineering Honors Society. After graduating from Binghamton and before going to law school, Andrew worked at Raytheon, a defense contractor, as a software engineer.

www.patentprofiler.com

Copyright 2019. All rights reserved.

www.ingramcontent.com/pod-product-compliance
Lightning Source LLC
Chambersburg PA
CBHW070336240526
45466CB00027B/2099